QUEEN OF HEARTS I AM

An Inspirational Handbook Perspective on
Identity, Authenticity, and Mindset

SPECIAL EDITION BY
GILDA F. JOHNSON

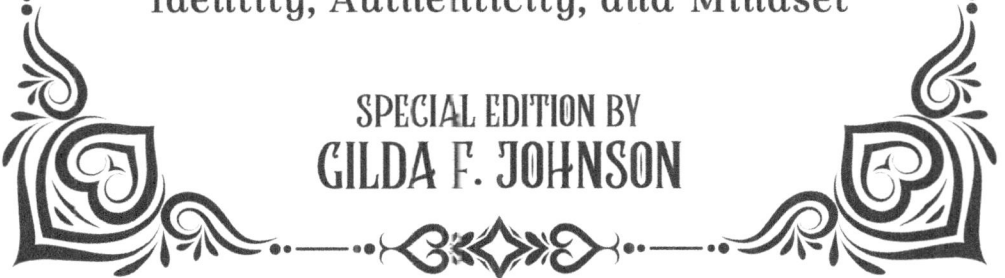

ACKNOWLEDGMENT

I first want to acknowledge, glorify, honor, and thank God for being the source of understanding of who I AM.

Secondly, I want to acknowledge my parents for being chosen to procreate and entrusted to nurture me and instill in me the principles and morals that define who I AM.

Third, I acknowledge my husband, Douglas P. Johnson, and my children for shaping me into the best version of myself, making it possible to fulfill my divine-given purpose and maximum potential as a human being.

Last, I want to acknowledge all readers who will read and embrace my message and affirm themselves in who they believe they are, and not by society's dictations.

DEDICATION

I dedicate this work to all who find themselves doubting their identity, questioning their true selves, or puzzled by the modern era of self-identification.

I also dedicate this book to my children: Gianne, Elijah, Emanussa, and Emanuel. It will be a love note to remind them when life feels unmanageable, their sense of identity can be found in their faith and community. If at any point in life, they experience a sense of loss or doubt about what constitutes an authentic self in their life trajectory, they will read this handbook, be mindful, and reflect on the I AM acronym.

This special edition is a reference point and foundation dedicated to all human existence. Reflecting on the simple three-point acronym I AM can be a life changer. First, the pronoun I stands for identity, and AM stands for who I AM; authenticity and mindset are core values to success. Second, true identity defines each human being. Third, a sense of being authentic is needed to succeed in life.

Additionally, I dedicate this work to God for creating me as I AM and choosing my parents, Maria and Jose A. F. Ferro, to help me develop and grow as the human being I AM.

Who do you say I AM?

Who do you think I AM?

Who do you see that I AM?

Who AM I?

TABLE OF CONTENTS

PREFACE

I AM is a special edition book that reflects on the ideology of identity, authenticity, and mindset and the author's perspective of what constitutes and defines identity in human beings.

I embarked on this ideology of Queen of Hearts Special Edition "I AM" due to the new era of controversial discussions and concerns about identity in today's world affecting all areas of life.

How can one be an instrument of change and live with confidence if their identity is lost or questioned? This is the question I continue asking myself as I analyze and observe the struggles of many. In my journey to understand today's issues with identity raised by the LGBTQ+ community – affecting the workplace, community, and all social media platforms – I came to question and reflect on who I am and for whom God created me to be a part of society.

Therefore, when I see people struggling with self-worth and self-identity, it has quickened me to inquire about these questions: how did I arrive at my conviction, and where have I gotten my belief of who I AM?

Many are hurting and struggling daily to be happy in their self-identity. It is an urgent quest for every human being to become an individual who brings value and their best to society and the community. Yet, how can happiness or the highest self come to fruition if the sense of identity is lost? The question became evident as I journeyed to acknowledge that it has been essential in all my life matters, including developing a professional working environment, relating to others, and understanding my place in the world. Therefore, it is imperative to recognize and know my worth and capabilities, who I believe I AM, and what I AM capable of doing and offering in this life through the scope of my sense of identity. Consequently, I invite the readers to embark on this quest, be accountable to their self-identity, and not lean on society's dictation to self-reidentify.

Author,

Gilda F. Johnson

INTRODUCTION

"I AM who I AM." - Exodus 3:14

God said to Moses, I AM WHO I AM. This is what you are to say to the Israelites: "I AM sent me to you." My question is, who are we to say we are? Who is behind our identity? Who should we say is the originator of our identity? Who was behind the first and foremost original being in our ancestral line? My answer is that there has to be a creator of the universe of all creations, including human beings. For me, God is the one and only master of my identity. Have you ever noticed that in every introduction of ourselves and every encounter, most of us say "I AM…" and then our name or "My name is…?" I ask you, as the reader, to pause and ask yourself: *Who Am I? What do others believe and say I AM?* It is fair for everyone to ask and reflect on these questions. Do an introspection and inquire about your essence in life. The answer is in you and not in the eyes of the beholder. For simplicity in understanding this quest on identity, authenticity, and mindset, I came to a simple definition of the acronym I AM.

I stands for *Identity*. The moment I realized that my identity was dictated before I was even born or formed in my mother's womb was pivotal to understanding that the family I belong to was not the first contact of my existence. My identity comes from God, who created everything, including my existence and all there is. Two scriptures spoke to me on this topic in my favorite book, the Bible. Jeremiah 1:5 says, "Before I formed you in the womb, I knew you." Additionally, it is stated, that I am "fearfully and wonderfully made in His image" (Psalm 139:14). Therefore, both you and I are made in His image.

A stands for *Authenticity*. God is a creative God, and He does not repeat His creations. Consequently, He created every one of us uniquely. There is no cloning or repetition. There is only one fingerprint of each human being who ever lived. That speaks very loudly to the perfection and precision in every design that came to God's thoughts. Therefore, knowing that our thoughts and ways are not God's thoughts and ways, it is wise to adhere to His counsel as Isaiah 55:8-9 says, "For my thoughts are not your thoughts, neither are your ways my ways,' declares the LORD." God's intentions and creativity toward humanity through His covenant are explicit. So, God created all living creatures of every kind and made a covenant with His creations.

M stands for *Mindset*. Romans 12:2 says, "Do not be conformed to this world, but be transformed by the renewing of your mind." God instructs us to have a growth mindset, evolving, growing, and exploring the creativity of our thoughts as heirs and mirror images of His thoughts.

- Gilda F. Johnson

CHAPTER I

IDENTITY

What is identity? How do we form and believe in our identity? As a Christian woman, my identity is in Christ Jesus. However, identity intertwines with the intrinsic nature of being and the environment. The blueprint book of life teaches that He knew me before I was even born. His intention was for good, to prosper me and not to harm me. Therefore, the spiritual life is first before my physical life. Consequently, identity is the foundation of our spiritual being. Human beings are made of body, mind, and spirit. It is incredible that parents are chosen before a human being's birth. Psalm 139:13-16 says, "For you created my inmost being; you knit me together in my mother's womb. I praise you because I am fearfully and wonderfully made; your works are wonderful, I know that full well." His eyes saw my unformed body. All the days ordained for me were written in His book. I am who I am for who He created me to be, not my perception of who I am or society dictates of who I am, for He formed me before I even knew my name.

Moreover, He plans to prosper and not harm us, as Jeremiah 29:11 says, "'For I know the plans I have for you,' declares the Lord, 'plans to prosper you and not to harm you, plans to give you hope and a future.'" Therefore, each human being was created for a purpose, put on Earth for a purpose on purpose, and placed here to live a prosperous life. Sometimes our vision and purpose can be misleading if not aligned with the divine purpose for God's perfect will. God is the one that holds the answers to the ultimate affair of each individual. John 4:24 says, "God is spirit, and his worshipers must worship in the spirit and truth." He is seeking those who worship Him in truth and spirit; He will reveal the utmost divine purpose to those who seek Him diligently. The form of worshiping required is to seek your fulfillment of the soul. Nevertheless, when seeking His kingdom first, all things will be added to life. As a spiritual being, there is no need to chase the things of this world because, in due timing, all things will come in God's will and appropriate time.

Identity is defined as being who or what a person is. The earlier one acknowledges and arrives at a sense of self-identification, the better poised they are to achieve life's purpose. Seek Him and your spiritual identity first when it still may be found. Think about Peter's story. Peter and the other fishermen were fishing all day and did not catch any fish throughout the whole day because the net was cast in the wrong spot. John 21:6 states that when the net was cast in the right place, "they were unable to haul the net in because of the large number of fish." This example is not to cast out your identity concerning your given loved ones but to gear you and mind-diving reflections on the original cause and effect of all things, including existence. For God does not just give life; He is life. Become observant and listen to the Universe; God is always speaking to His people and creations. All the answers to all there is and to all there will be is right within everyone.

When one's identity is acknowledged and manifested, it builds the self-core foundation that becomes the essence of life. With a solid foundation, everything becomes clear like crystal clear water, and confidence rises. Identity dictates authenticity, which builds the confidence needed to excel and become extraordinary human beings. The uniqueness, value, and purpose of life originate from within.

Working in a non-profit agency, I was amazed daily by emails with co-workers identifying themselves as a pronoun (e.g., I use the pronoun he, his, him, her, hers, they, them) and then asking what pronouns I use. My reaction was to answer the question by inquiring about myself and the inner thoughts of my own beliefs. Reflecting on the matter's effect on my core values and principles propelled me to stand on my convictions against approaches of identity which has become prevalent among others. I considered how it had become common to inquire about someone's identity through a pronoun. Eventually, I came to the conviction through my faith and belief that my pronoun is and has always been I AM and ME, who God created me to be. Nothing or any new era approach to the matter can change my identity or the essence of who I am and who I am to be in the world. No construct dictated by the world can change human identity. Neither can the framework approach be dictated by others in the face of the one that created me before I was formed in my mother's womb. This approach gave me a sense of closure to acknowledging pronoun usage by identifying myself as I AM and I AM ME and, unapologetically, a positive disruptor to shift the current norm standing out as God's creation. The new trend on how to identify myself does not align with the essence of my being. I refused to be conformed by the things of this world, to adapt to a new way of identification, and not allow myself to investigate my inner being and thoughts freely.

Furthermore, I ponder on the lamin, the minuscule protein cell that forms the construct of human DNA, which, when observed under a microscope, has been viewed as the form of a cross. Scientists have been amazed by this. It may be a mere coincidence. Some may say that nothing is a coincidence because there is no such coincidence but the divine orchestration of the Universe by a creator. Whatever may be conceived or perceived, human minds have the permission to wonder and make their conclusion about the creation and its maker.

When life was not focused on identity

Growing up, I always loved to do what I felt made me happy and lived a life of enjoyment. There was never a moment I could remember trying to think of who I am or what pronoun I should use to identify myself. However, I enjoyed doing certain sports considered more masculine than feminine at some point in my life. I could have passed as a so-called "tomboy." Nevertheless, as I grew older, I became more feminine to the fullest and enjoyed being a female in all the essence of the definition of a female. Finally, I became an adult fully formed and identified myself as a woman. I procreated and nurtured four biological children, married, and lived as I believed a woman should live. It has been an excellent fifty-four years of life embracing my femininity and learning from my imperfections and failures that paved the way to success. Although I am a feminist in all its essence, I respect the opposite sex and others within society and community that identify as otherwise. So, my question is this: what is the issue now? What is the need for identity reaffirmation? When did identity become an issue and sparked my interest in addressing it? The truth is there has been a movement of expression seeking self-identification and inclusion rights in the past years.

When identity became an issue in the eyes of the beholder

Little did I know that sometime around 2020, I became aware that I was constantly being invited to adapt or address myself through a pronoun in my professional environment and community. I have identified myself throughout my life as my name and my position within a female gender. I never perceived a need to affirm my identity. However, it surprised me that in the eyes of others, there was an urgency to re-identify myself to fit the new culture of pronouns. In all respect, I determined the reasons behind the urgent invitation and the dilemma behind this quest. I came to respect those from the LGBTQ+ community, and the difficulty, and ordeal of their life trajectory. At the same time, I did not feel there was an urgent personal need to adjust myself to the culture. So I embarked on my quest: why should I settle for what others dictate instead of adhering to my inner conviction? All I need to be, represent, and succeed is within me. Consequently, I stand by my Christian values. I am a predestined, self-identified female who doesn't need to present myself as the new trend would like me to do. Claiming that I am who God created me to be is a sufficient stance on the matter. It is a human right to choose freely. Consequently, feeling content in my fifty-four years of identification was sufficient, and I lacked any need to reaffirm myself to the social trend of using a pronoun. However, not including myself in this new way to identify at work or in the community came with a cause and effect.

How I felt/how life shifted in relation to identity

In my four years and four months working in a non-profit family service job, I felt isolated and targeted for not going along with the pronoun identification culture. I became a target. I was questioned multiple times about why I was using I AM and ME instead of the other common pronouns used by colleagues and those specified in the

LGBTQ+ community. This reaction from the leaders and staff members of the agency was one of my stances that were perceived as a pattern of unprofessional behavior on my part that did not fit the mission and values of this agency that pretended to be an all-inclusive place of work. How can a workplace claim inclusion when my human rights were being denied and the free will to choose how to address myself and identify myself was challenged and viewed as defiant behavior? This reaction stirred a conviction within me to overcome the situation.

How I overcame the Identity dilemma at work/community

I overcame the situation by continuing to stand in my truth and beliefs until my last day in the position. I was forced to reaffirm, standing in my truth and God-given identity that cannot be shaken. It brought me peace to stand for my beliefs. I will continue respecting all human beings regardless of their gender or approaches to identity. God's will is to love others and refrain from judging even when my convictions and beliefs are misunderstood or misinterpreted. I am fully aware I can only change the things I can change and accept the things I cannot change; because knowing the difference is wisdom. Overcoming means remaining peaceful with my convictions while respecting differences. Victory can only be measured when one can agree to disagree with others yet still live in a unified, harmonious world by accepting that only some may think alike. However, this calls for self-reflection on the matter.

Looking back, reflecting on how I feel

I don't think I would have reacted differently or used the agency pronoun approaches as the culture permitted. I may have sometimes used silence instead of exercising my rights and standing on the matter. At times the lesson learned is that there was no progress in making my point and persuading others of my convictions. Yet, there is no greater agony than not standing for your truth and beliefs. To disregard self-identity and its relatable aspect is dangerous. It leaves an open field of wonder and uncertainty about the essence of my being. Reflecting on either stance, I pondered, what my name means in the old English dictionary. My name means golden or gilded, meaning covered by gold, which one may think has an eloquent meaning. However, I see it as continuously being refined by fire as gold in my life experiences, and this experience was not any different. Therefore, I invite the reader to be inspired and encouraged to stand on their truth no matter the counterfeiting experienced along life's journey.

Words of encouragement to others about identity reflection

My words of encouragement to others are to stand in your truth and not wave the universal truth of I AM. No one can rob the inborn dignity and essence of another's life. Each individual only has one life to live. So live it well to the best of your potential because you are entitled to your life account. Nelson Mandela said it this way: "They can strip you of everything, but the only thing no one can take away from you is your dignity because dignity is an inborn quality that belongs only to the individual given at birth."

If you cannot be what your thoughts and dreams ask of you, at least be your true self. There is no other person like you. All others have been taken. Therefore, embrace your true identity to achieve your best potential on Earth.

Write three sentences to describe your Identity:

Make a note to yourself about the importance of Identity in your life and its correlation to the world:

CHAPTER II

AUTHENTICITY

"I praise you because I am fearfully and wonderfully made."

- Psalm 139:14

There is only one fingerprint for every human being in existence. Being authentic means, one acts in ways that show true self and feelings. Rather than showing people only a particular side of yourself, you express your whole self genuinely, not portions of yourself, to conform to the expectations of others. To succeed in being authentic, you first must know your true self according to your innermost being and principles correlated with a nurturing environment. Therefore, knowing your identity is crucial in expressing authenticity. Brene Brown says, "To be authentic, we must cultivate the courage to be imperfect – and vulnerable. We have to believe that we are fundamentally worthy of love and acceptance, just as we are. I've learned that there is no better way to invite more grace, gratitude, and joy into our lives than by mindfully practicing authenticity."[1] Authenticity is living with conviction and confidence, staying true to self, and not persuading or acting according to the expectations or acceptance of others. To be authentic or to thrive, one needs to be honest, trustworthy, and kind to self and the people around us.

An essential element of authenticity is integrity by being original, organic, and genuine toward others. Remember, God created only one of a kind for each type of creation. Each person has only one fingerprint; the precise and all-knowing God was behind our DNA construct.

---

[1] How to Be Yourself, Even in Life's Most Anxiety-Inducing Moments, Accessed on 12/8/2022.

Therefore, we are all endowed with unique aspects and characters. Within humankind, we all may carry similarities; however, the difference in expression and traits makes one unique and different.

There are five virtues for obtaining an understanding of one's authenticity:

1. *Be true to yourself.* As Oscar Wilde famously said, "Be yourself; everyone else is already taken."[2] For example, you don't need to look at others or require others' acceptance to believe in and manifest who you are.

2. *Think inward, look outward.* Authentic individuals are deep thinkers who generate thoughts of power within and transfer them outward to add value to the lives of others.

3. *Treat people with kindness and respect.* As Henry James says, "Three things in human life that are important. The first is to be kind. The second is to be kind. And the third is to be kind." We all feel terrible when we are disrespected and even violated, so be kind to those around you. A simple act of kindness boosts your happiness and the receiver's happiness. Random acts of kindness can be the essence of supportive social relationships and build trust and compassion among individuals in a community.

4. *Be a great listener.* James 1:19 says, "Be quick to listen, slow to speak, and slow to become angry." The Chinese symbol for the verb "to listen" (聽 = ting) effectively illustrates what's involved when you're completely engaged in listening (Fig. 1). The character for ting features within it the symbols for ear, heart, and singular focus. To listen with ting requires eyes, ears, heart, and divine attention. For instance, in listening with eyes, it is vital to look into the eyes of the person speaking; in listening with ears, one must listen to the words expressed with acknowledgment of what is being said; divine attention means attending to what is being said and with the heart meaning to have empathy to the subject is being communicated. Consequently, genuinely listening enables us to hold a much higher quality of conversation and communication. We become more engaged and intentional about what the other person is saying. This deliberate act

[2] Online quote. https://quoteinvestigator.com/2014/01/20/be-yourself/. Accessed on 12/2022

enables deep listening skills when we bring heart, mind, ears, eyes, and divine attention to the table. This illustration of the symbol ting captures the real listening spirit (see Fig.1). Human beings were created for relationships built through communication and the authenticity of each individual. The act of listening is an essential element in building authentic relationships based on understanding our authentic selves.

5. *Authenticity is open-mindedness and fairness toward opportunities and people.* "Open your eyes to the beauty around you, open your mind to the wonders of life, open your heart to those who love you, and always be true to yourself," says Donna Davis. Open-mindedness is being truthful to self, having faith, and accepting a call to action. Authentic individuals are open-minded to new ideas. One may live by a code of values and morals that remain constant. However, when it comes to opinions, people, and events, authentic people are always open to listening, free of bias or preconceptions, and refraining from judging. It requires honesty, humility, and an understanding that humans are imperfect. No one who has ever lived has come close to perfection. Only God is perfect.

To live as an authentic self is to be watchful of your thoughts, words, and actions that can change and positively influence the world. Remain true to your personality, values, and spirit regardless of the pressure that you're under before you act. I discussed in the identity section that to be authentic means being unique. You are being authentic by embracing uniqueness while acknowledging faults and imperfections. It means loving yourself and others through kindness, compassion, listening, and valuing every experience, listening to their inner voices and instincts to maintain core values and morals rather than to persuade or become people pleasers. According to psychologists, on Psychology Today journal, being authentic and "real" is how you behave on the outside and matches how you feel on the inside, regardless of personal or social consequences.[3] So, be honest, be authentic, be you, and let your true self shine bright in the world because there is only one kind of you. Remember, you are unique, "fearfully, and wonderfully made" in the image of God, according to Psalm 139:14.

---

[3] The enigma of being yourself: A critical examination of the concept of authenticity. By Katrina P. Longman-Sereno and Mark R. Leary. First published online April 26, 2019.

Consequently, "Let love be genuine. Abhor what is evil; hold fast to what is good" (Romans 12:9 ESV). Be genuine, authentic, and unapologetic because there is only one version of you. The urgency for me to be authentic came to fruition when I realized that a person could only achieve success and happiness when they thrive on being authentic, regardless of being liked or accepted. It is "works" in vain to be anything else but you. I realized it is impossible to please everyone, and no matter how good you may be, there is no complete satisfaction in the eyes of the beholder. Therefore, it is an impossible mission to attempt to please everyone. Consequently, it is better to live an authentic, genuine, organic life and achieve success and happiness with self. This state yields to make others happy as well.

Nevertheless, be kind and loving regardless of mistreatment and expectation from others and without expecting acceptance from others. Every human wants validation, reassurance that they are loved, and to know they matter. In a speech to Harvard graduates, Oprah Winfrey says it this way: "You will find true success and happiness if you have only one goal: to fulfill the highest, most truthful expression of yourself as a human being." You want to maximize your personality by using your energy to lift yourself, your family, and the people around you. The most critical lesson Oprah learned in the many years of her career talking to people is the following: There is a common denominator to all of us. We want to be validated. We want to be understood. Oprah said during interviews on her show that as soon as the camera shuts off, everyone turns to her and asks her this question: *Was that ok?* She learned from President Bush, Barack Obama, Beyonce, heroes perpetrators of crimes, friends, family, enemies, and strangers in every argument, every encounter, and every exchange. We all want to know one thing: *Did you hear me? Did you see me? Did what I said mean anything to you?* It is imperative to embrace authenticity to be the true self to others in the world with the intention not to lose the ability to understand and stand in somebody else's shoes and to recognize that we have more similarities than differences within our uniqueness. The most basic traces are the same variables of emotions that constitute happiness. Such as that, we all demonstrate happiness or sadness in the same way. These emotions' outward physical projection can be a smile of joy, laughter, a sad face, or crying. Oprah Winfrey said this after imitating Barbara Walters in her early years of broadcasting. It is better to be the best authentic self than to be anybody else. For you only know the surface of others. In summary, there is only one of you and only one of me. Therefore, be yourself and thrive on being the best version of yourself. And if everything else fails, be kind.[4]

Authenticity Questionnaire Tool

1. Are you true to yourself with others?

2. Do you hide any traits of who you are when you are with others?

3. Do you have integrity with yourself as well as with others?

4. Do you stand to your truth regardless of whether others agree with you?

5. Are you a people pleaser?

6. Do you feel comfortable expressing yourself?

7. Is it more important to you to do what is right or to follow the crowd?

When life was not focused on authenticity

I think about my journey and ponder my authentic struggles. I consider and ask myself, *Have I been authentic all my life?* The answer is no. I have to accept I was not always genuine in accepting myself for who I was created to be and embracing the real me. I remember times of being a people pleaser, attempting to be someone who others would most likely accept. I yielded to the perception of acceptance of others at times and felt like acting to please others and be included. However, it was a lot of work, and I struggled as time passed and grew older and wiser. My question to that younger me is this: *Did I achieve what I expected by being what others expected of me? Did I express the essence of my being?* The answer is no. I did not necessarily achieve the means to forfeit who I am—consequently, I felt the craving to fulfill the void by being organic and generic in my uniqueness. If the end means of the game are not

---

[4] Oprah Winfrey Harvard Commencement speech. Online access on November, 2022

met, what is the purpose of acting it out? Finally, I flipped the switch. The realization is that, in the long run, the benefits of being authentic outweigh the result of pleasing others through pretenses.

When authenticity became intentional

Nevertheless, the realization or the "aha" moment revealed that being authentic requires less work and less effort. There is freedom and contentment in striving to be the person I was created to be and only working on self-progress and fulfillment. I put intention toward becoming the best version of myself and not losing focus on the work from within rather than from outside sources, including others' perceptions and misconceptions of who I should be to be accepted or likable. The freedom and effortless work paved the way to no more compromises on my authenticity.

How I felt/how life shifted in relation to authenticity

My life completely shifted as I felt freedom and a release from the prison of the mind. I was no more tied to unnecessary ideology chains. Realizing that it is better to be my authentic self with flaws and imperfections liberated me. I know only the surface of someone else. I can never know what anyone is like or be of anyone's liking, but I can thrive by being a better human being while on earth. The goal was to succeed in being a better self each day and focusing on the refined product at the end of my life journey.

How I overcame the lack of authenticity

I overcame by yielding to the source of light in my life by being grounded in the blueprint book, which has taught me the right and wrong characteristics to foster to be my unique self but toward a higher self-created in the image of God. I now commit to relentless refusal to abide by systems and dictations of how one should behave to be acceptable instead of working on the inside out and not vice versa. I am living in truth as I shall be free if the truth is meant to set me free. The Bible says in this world, we will have trials and tribulations, but Jesus has overcome them; therefore, being in Christ, we are overcomers. I unapologetically choose to be organic and genuine regardless of the acceptance of others or be likable.

Looking back, reflecting on my thoughts

Looking back, the lessons I learned helped me change my life trajectory by continuing to thrive on living a life of contentment in all circumstances and being unapologetic, intentionally moving toward my innermost being and growth toward a divine purpose. It was worth the journey if I had to go through all of it to be who I am today, it was all worth the journey. I am the only one responsible for choosing to live and leave a mark on my descendants. To earnestly seek my divine purpose and fulfillment in life is a desire that my creator has deposited in me since I was born. It is okay that many distractions were present on the way. What matters most is that I refocused and fixed my eyes on the goal of my humanity agenda predestined to be on the earth. There is no such thing as "too late." The opportunities are endless, and the chances never run out. The difference is to deliberately seek the authenticity required to achieve the divine role that only I was created to deliver to the world.

Words of encouragement to others about authenticity

My words of encouragement to others are to be your true self regardless of imperfections or others' perceptions. It is worthwhile, and there is only gain. You were perfectly made to be who you are as one of a kind. Everything needed is within. Nothing outward can change the innermost construct.

Suppose I can change the reader's time to refrain from the vain pursuit of being a pleaser of others by living a life lacking authenticity, then it is my honor to communicate the value of achieving happiness and true self-worth uniquely designated for you. I can consider sharing this message a success in itself.

Write three core values that constitute authenticity:

....

....

....

....

What characteristics make you authentic?

....

....

....

....

What barriers block your authenticity?

....

....

....

....

List three tips for maintaining authenticity:

CHAPTER III

MINDSET

"Do not conform to the pattern of this world, but be transformed by renewing of your mind."-Romans 12:2 NIV

Mindset is a set of beliefs that shape how you make sense of the world and self-identity. There are two essential mindsets: the fixed mindset and the growth mindset. The fixed mindset believes abilities are fixed traits and cannot change and that talents and intelligence alone lead to success.

On the other hand, the growth mindset believes that talents and abilities can develop over time through effort and persistence. Of course, those who fall in the growth mindset category do not necessarily think they will become a modern Albert Einstein or Mozart just because they put in the effort and persisted enough. Nevertheless, everyone can be more intelligent or talented if they work toward a particular purpose and focus with persistence. Les Brown, a great motivational speaker, says, "A lot of people become discouraged too soon. The name of the game is you've got to be relentless." You do not quit until you win, so persist toward goals and strive to finish. There are no successes without failures. Failures are not the opposite of success but agents that will help progress toward success. Most successful individuals talk about their failures; however, they are persistent in repeatedly trying until they reach the goal. Martin Luther King, Jr. gave an analogy of persistence: "If you can't fly, then run. If you can't run, then walk. If you can't walk, then crawl, but whatever you do, you have to keep moving forward." I say believe and have faith, and everything is possible. Faith and belief move mountains. However, it is crucial to believe in the self first within the divine strength given by the source of light and power.

Fixed Mindset	*Growth Mindset*
1. Either I am good at it or not.	1. I can learn to do anything I want.
2. That's just who I am; I can't change it.	2. I am constantly evolving in progress.
3. If you have to work hard, you don't have the ability.	3. The more you challenge yourself, the wiser you become.
4. If I don't try, then I won't fail.	4. I only fail when I stop trying.
5. That job position is totally out of my league.	5. That job position looks challenging. Let me apply for it.

The mindset is critical for coping with life's challenges. When an individual has a growth mindset, the individual is unstoppable and has a hunger to learn, discover new things, and work hard through challenges. However, an individual with a fixed mindset is more likely to give up amid challenging circumstances. In the book Mindset: The New Psychology of Success, Dr. Carol Dweck claims that individuals with fixed mindsets seek validation to prove their worth to others and themselves.[5]

Growing up, I've seen so many individuals with the all-consuming urge to prove themselves in the classroom, their careers, and their relationships. Every situation calls for a confirmation of intellect, personality, or character. *Will I succeed or fail in this situation? Will I look smart or dumb? Will I be accepted or rejected? Will I feel like a winner or a loser?*

The following questionnaire is a tool to reflect and decide which type of mindset you fall into. Then, for each statement, determine whether you agree or disagree.

1. I am born with a certain IQ; consequently, it is fixed at birth and unable to be changed.

2. My basic abilities and personality cannot improve or be changed no matter what I do.

3. People can change if it is their will and intention.

---

[5] Mindset: The New Psychology of Success, Carol Dweck, Online Accessed on November, 2022

4. You can improve your IQ and learn new things.

5. People either have particular talents or don't. Therefore, you can't acquire new skills.

6. Studying, working hard, and practicing new skills are all ways to develop new talents and abilities.

If you agree mostly with statements 1, 2, and 5, then the probability is that you have a fixed mindset. On the other hand, if you agree mostly with 3, 4, and 6, you tend to have a growth mindset.

To unfix a fixed mindset, consider the following suggestions:

- Focus on the journey. See the value in your journey regardless of obstacles. Don't miss out on lessons within the process by focusing only on the end goal.

- When faced with a task, be mindful that you haven't mastered it. Integrate your intentions to accomplish the task by overcoming any obstacles. We will have trials and tribulations, but we are overcomers, conquerors, victorious, and triumphant because Jesus has overcome our troubles.

- There is power in words; there is death and life in the power of the tongue (Proverbs 18:21). So, be watchful of your words and thoughts. Replace negative thoughts and statements with positive ideas and comments. This simple exercise will move individuals from a fixed mindset to a growth mindset that leads to a transformed mind.

- Challenges can be lessons through the learning process. So, embrace challenges and take away wisdom from the experiences.

Suppose you fall into a fixed mindset that interferes with fulfilling your God-given purpose in life. Then, take a step back, reflect, and consider the growth mindset versus the fixed mindset. The mindset is like a thermostat and can move an individual to take action and thrive for the imminent outcome of human potential. Napoleon Hill says, "If a man can conceive and believe, he can achieve." Likewise, the mind has the potential to spark inner desires that manifest outward through actions through a growth mindset. So, I ask you, the reader, to reexamine these perspectives and consider the type suitable for your current life trajectory.

How was Life without mindset awareness?

I never did put so many thoughts into a mindset perspective in my life. I was unaware my mindset or my set of thoughts and ideas dictated my life. I never questioned my mind's thoughts or evaluated them by intentionally considering mindset type, whether mine was fixed, growth, or a mix of both. Not knowing what needed to be changed, I did not change anything in my approach to life. Additionally, I did not perceive any need to analyze my type of mindset and inquire if I would want to change it if it meant a life-changing course for the betterment of my life.

When did mindset become a game-changer?

The idea of mindset awareness became prevalent when my life changed. I was diagnosed with stage three breast cancer and came to face the idea that my life could be short or even death was a possibility. I then asked this question: *If today was my last day on earth, would I leave satisfied, and if not, what is one thing I must do before I depart?* That is to live without fear and to do everything I desired as if it was the last day on earth. If I fail at anything, I set my mind to do, at least I tried. *What is the worst that can happen to me if whatever I attempt or try fails?* In reality, the consequences of not trying are more significant than trying and falling short. This reflection pushed me from my comfort zone and explored why I was stuck in my beliefs and mindset. Finally, I realized that the Bible, my source of guidance in life, says it this way in Romans 12:2, "Do not conform to the pattern of this world but be transformed by the renewing of your mind." Therefore, we are commanded not to conform to what we know and the things our environment offers but to expand our horizons and constantly reach for transformation.

What difference does mindset evoke in my life?

This mindset shift made all the difference in my current life. I demolished the wall and defeated the lack of ability to pursue dreams and visions without barriers or pre-set beliefs. Les Brown says, "If you fall, fall on your back. If you can look up, you can get up." So, I took his advice and went forth, trying to achieve the goals I set ahead of me regardless of obstacles or trials. I will continue to live relentlessly, pursuing my innermost dreams and visions deposited in my heart by my creator, and fearlessly keep moving until I win through my life's trajectory.

How did I shift my mindset?

My mindset shifted, so I no longer looked at my circumstances to seek my goals. Instead, I research and find ways to solve the problems that prevent me from achieving my goals. I intentionally focus on the goal and end product, asking my spiritual guide to direct my steps and act until the goal is complete. I became unstuck by my circumstances and believed that "all things are possible through Christ who strengthened me"(Philippians 4:13) and applied this concept in my life, not just reciting the scripture. What circumstances are preventing you from reaching your goals? Look around and ask yourself, *How can it be achieved? Are there others who have completed it? How did the successful individual achieve it?* Investigate and educate yourself about the matter. Then follow the steps and framework to take action toward the goal in mind.

Reflecting on my mindset evolution

Reader, you may wonder if I have mastered the mindset skills for a complete growth mindset. My answer is no. The shift from a fixed to a growth mindset is a dynamic trajectory. It fluctuates. The difference is to be aware and act upon it when it does not serve a purpose within a life well worth living. I constantly find myself in a battle of the mind. Nevertheless, I am determined to win that battle and not let it cripple me from doing what I want. To do anything less may lead to regret later on in life. It's a continuous effort to progress and not become fixed in my mindset.

Words of encouragement to readers on mindset

Do not be dismayed or deceived. On the contrary, be encouraged and of good cheer that there will be harvest in its due time. "As long as the earth endures, seed time and harvest, cold and heat, summer, and winter, day and night will never cease" (Genesis 8:22). The mind is like a garden. You will plant a seed, and it will grow good or bad fruit. The fruit's outcome depends on pruning and watering. I invite you to consider your mindset and consider the advantages or disadvantages. It only starts with taking action and analyzing our thoughts, ideas, and beliefs. Everything needed for success is within. However, every thought, idea, and dream remains a dream without actions. Success yields from effort, persistence, consistency, and the willingness to do the work required to achieve the goals set throughout life's journey.

What is your type of mindset, and why?

Write three goals toward a growth mindset:

....

....

....

....

How important do you believe mindset is to achieving goals, and why?

....

....

....

....

Describe moments of fixed mindset versus growth mindset:

....

....

....

....

CHAPTER IV

I AM ACRONYM AFFIRMATIONS

After reflecting on the acronym, I AM, I invite you to apply it in your journey by repeating affirmations at least once a week to reflect on who you are and the core values of your essence. It is an individual exercise at times deemed appropriate to do the exercise and be mindful of what constitutes the essence of being who you are as a human being and your contribution to the world.

I AM unstoppable

I AM successful

I AM kind

I AM generous

I AM beautiful

I AM_____

I AM_____

I AM_____

I AM_____

I AM_____

I AM_____

I AM_____

I AM_____

I AM_____

I AM_____

I AM_____

I AM_____

I AM_____

I AM_____

I AM_____

I AM_____

I AM_____

I AM_____

The above exercise aims to give self permission to believe in self first as a step toward accomplishing tasks that may be diverted due to imposter syndrome. Imposter syndrome is believing thoughts are controlled by circumstances that may not be the reality of individual potential. Consequently, this exercise is not to boost superego behaviors or self-centeredness that would defeat the purpose of dreams and visions but a cause that is greater than self, goodness toward others, and impact the lives of others through service.

CHAPTER V

MANIFESTATION - CALL TO ACTION

Manifestation is simply a call to action. Dreams and visions were divinely given to all that dream. A life worth living is one in which dreams are allowed, and the ambition of achieving the best life has to offer is the ultimate goal for every human being. However, if dreams or visions are without actions, they just remain a dream or vision lost in thoughts and unfulfillment of a life trajectory. For dreams and ideas to come to fruition, they need actions that are intentional toward the outward manifestation of the dream or vision. Consequently, acknowledging the identity, authenticity, and shifting mindset that allows personal growth is just a first step. The second step is to act intentionally to activate and manifest the dream. Only then the dream or vision becomes alive and active.

There are a couple of tips to make dreams into action. First, write them plain and trace a plan. Abraham Lincoln says, "If you fail to plan, you plan to fail." So write your dream, plan it well, strategize your plan of deliverance, and fearlessly complete tasks and goals toward the dream.

Write down the reason or reasons for the achievement of a goal:

....

....

....

What is the desired outcome after achieving the goal?

....

....

....

How essential is it to your divine purpose to complete the goal? Why?

....

....

....

On a scale from 0 to 10, how important is it to complete the goal?

(0) (1) (2) (3) (4) (5) (6) (7) (8) (9) (10)

CHAPTER VI

MOTIVATION QUOTES

According to the Oxford dictionary, motivation is derived from the word 'motive,' which denotes a person's needs, wants, or urges. It is merely the process of motivating individuals to action in order to achieve goals. Additionally, motivation is the psychological element fueling people's behavior in the context of goal setting. Moreover, it is the reason or reasons one has for acting or behaving in a particular way.

The following are some quotes that I read periodically to inspire and keep me moving toward my goals:

- "Nothing can defeat you unless you consent to be defeated."
  - Gilda F. Johnson

- " I feel enormous gratitude that I've found my calling."
  - Gilda F. Johnson

- "Suddenly, everything came together for me. I saw that my name is an inseparable part of my essence, and this gave me great joy."
  - Gilda F. Johnson

- "It is important to be aware of the choices we make in life and not to feel like a victim of circumstances."
  - Leah Hartman

- "Today, I don't define myself through my career. I define myself through my home. My complete restoration was about redefining my identity in Christ."
  - Gilda F. Johnson

- "Without water, without air, how long can you survive? That's how I feel about my faith in God."
  - Gilda F. Johnson

- "If today was the last day on earth, would you leave satisfied? If not, what is one thing you must do before you depart and be satisfied?"
  - Gilda F. Johnson

- "Lately, I have chosen to direct my energy solely toward women. The understanding is that women are very strong and powerful yet oppressed and weakened. A deep desire in me stirred up to raise women's strength to rise and conquer."
  - Gilda F. Johnson

- "I find myself dealing with what is in front of me here and now, but sometimes my focus is on the essence of it all. I sense that it's something much bigger than me."
  - Gilda F. Johnson

- "Every day, I get angry, and upset, and there are disagreements and fights…but the way I see it, this is a life lived with others. I don't look at it as a hardship but as an integral part of life. If everything is fine all the time, then something is wrong."
  - Adi Levi

- "There is a human there. There is who they are on the inside. There is emotion. There is beauty. That is what I am seeking."
  - Tamar Kinarty

- "I can do all things through Christ which strengtheneth me."
  - Philippians 4:13

I invite the reader to keep a journal of quotes or inspirational statements that motivates and helps to progress in seeking dreams or visions.

CHAPTER VII

IMPOSTER SYNDROME

What is Imposter Syndrome?

According to the Oxford dictionary, imposter syndrome is "the persistent inability to believe that one's success is deserved or has been legitimately achieved as a result of one's efforts or skills." For me, imposter syndrome is a third party or thought attempting to influence my essence, and born rights are given capabilities to achieve what my mind can conceive and believe in myself, God-given gifts, or inborn talents.

What are the signs of being aware of IS?

There are many signs to watch for and prevent one from falling into the imposter syndrome dilemma. However, to be aware of the fact is a step ahead of the game to win over goal setting.

Tips on how to overcome Imposter Syndrome?

To overcome imposter syndrome, be aware and acknowledge it as a setback item if not dealt with appropriately. Second, focus on the task set ahead and not on the abilities. Third, find out who had done the task before you and accomplished the task. There is no secret to success. There is a formula or steps used to complete tasks. Fourth, set small goals for the project plan. Finally, work toward the plan until it is complete.

While reflecting on our identity, authenticity, and mindset, it is fair to say that self-doubt is just a negative thought that can become a roadblock to achieving dreams. However, when one battles self-doubt, one knows that what one believes, conceives it, and knows it can be achieved.

Therefore, it is essential to believe in self first.

Imposter Syndrome Questionnaire:

Write down great successful tasks achieved:

....

....

....

Write down at least three characteristics that were helpful in achieving tasks:

....

....

....

What negative thoughts needed to be overridden or dealt with to achieve tasks?

....

....

....

How satisfied were you with the accomplishment of tasks?

(1) (2) (3) (4) (5) (6) (7) (8) (9) (10)

Unsatisfied   Satisfied   Very Satisfied

How much of the achievement of tasks did you attribute to efforts?

(1) (2) (3) (4) (5) (6) (7) (8) (9) (10)

Not at all   A little   A lot

Additionally, a resource to consider is found at the Clance IP Scale, developed by Pauline Rose Clance; you can take the test to determine whether or not you have IP characteristics. Go to

http://www.paulineroseclance.com

CHAPTER VIII

I AM AN ACRONYM TEMPLATE

Upon completing previous chapters and questionnaires, I invite the reader to personalize these three core values set of the acronym, I AM for identity, authenticity, and mindset growth. This template can be helpful as a daily or weekly routine to recite and reflect on the path and life goals achieved toward the individual purpose.

Specify Three Core Value adjectives for personalized Identity:

....

....

....

Specify Three Core Value adjectives for personalized Authenticity:

....

....

....

Specify Three Core Value steps for personalized Mindset Growth:

....

....

....

From 0 to 10, how intentionally were the core values applied to the life purpose journey?

(0) (1) (2) (3) (4) (5) (6) (7) (8) (9) (10)

CONCLUSION

With a grateful heart, I write this book to freely express my thoughts and emotions toward the new era of popularity in manifestations of identity. This handbook is interactive and with four goals in mind. First and foremost, it was written to *spark the curiosity* in others to reflect on their identity and perceive it as the foundation for success in life. "In the beginning, God created the heavens and earth" (Genesis 1:1). "In the beginning was the word and the word was with God, and the Word is God" (John 1:1). This book is just *words to express my conviction* and beliefs on my identity and reach those who freely want to read my perspective on this matter. The human being's identity is the foundation and *the essence of success* and happiness. All inborn characteristics of individuals can be molded and diverted by the nurturing environment; however, as human beings, we have free will to choose and accept the interlaced work of nature versus nurture without dismissing the origin of such. As a Christian woman, the conviction of my pronoun is I AM who God created ME to be, and regardless of other beliefs, it is my right as a human being to stand for my truth without apologies. I am free to embrace my truth, and attempting to understand new era identification ideology does not mean robbing my rights or silencing my voice and expression.

Therefore, the acronym I AM is simply a gesture to understand my truth and make it known to those with an open heart to listen and reflect on my perspective: I AM for identity, authenticity, and mindset.

ABOUT THE AUTHOR

Gilda is a three-time international Amazon Best-Selling author, a life coach, and a wife happily married to Douglas P. Johnson. She is a mother of four children: Gianne, Elijah, Emanussa, and Emanuel. Gilda is a Jesus lover and a peacemaker. She is a transformational spiritual speaker known as Goldy for being refined by fire like gold. She is a Queen of Hearts International life coach to transform and heal women's hearts through inspiring, encouraging, and enlightening mindsets by equipping, educating, and leading women toward their divine purpose. The Queen of Hearts Life Coaching is to reach 1,000 women worldwide in the first three years and build a collaborative movement of successful, driven, triumphant women who overcame trials and tribulations in life. Gilda has a Bachelor's degree in Psychology with a concentration in Alcohol and Addiction Studies from the University of Rhode Island, a Master's degree in Arts and Ministry, and post-graduate studies in Divinity from Liberty University. In addition, Gilda has a decade of research studies at Brown University on addictive behaviors and the environmental interaction with epigenetics through the Rhode Island Children Studies. Lastly, Gilda is the co-founder of Ruach Hakodesh-Holy Spirit Ministry and Bible Restorative Table Talk, which aims to discuss biblical or non-biblical topics through the lenses of the Bible.

REFERENCES

1. *Holy Bible. New International Version, Zondervan Publishing House, 2012.*

2. *Growth mindset. What it is. What to cultivate. By Carol Dweck. 2017 Mindset Works, Inc.*

3. *Mindset survey, go to https://blog.mindsetworks.com/what-s-my-mindset, Accessed on September, 2022.*

4. *The Impostor Phenomenon: When Success Makes you feel Like a Fake (pp. 20-22), by P.R. Clance, 1985, Toronto: Bantam Books, Copyright 1985 by Pauline Rose Clance, Ph.D. ABPP. Accessed on December, 2022.*

5. *OED Accessed Online. Oxford University Press, September 2022. Web. 5 December 2022.*

6. *Ting Picture, Cc.https://ar.pinterest.com/pin/601089881491030002/, Accessed on November, 2022.*

7. *How to Be Yourself, Even in Life's Most Anxiety-Inducing Moments, https://www.oprah.com/spirit/brene-brown-advice-how-to-be-yourself/all, Accessed on November, 2022.*

8. *Mindset: The New Psychology of Success, Carol Dweck, Accessed on September, 2022.*

9. *The enigma of being yourself: A critical examination of the concept of authenticity. By Katrina P. Longman-Sereno and Mark R. Leary. First published online on April 26, 2019. https://journals.sagepub.com/doi/full/10.1037/gpr0000157, Accessed online on 1/14/2023.*

10. *Oprah Winfrey Harvard Commencement speech. At https://www.youtube.com/watch?v=GMWFieBGR7c, Accessed online on November, 2022*

APPENDIX

Illustration Credit

"TING"
(to listen)

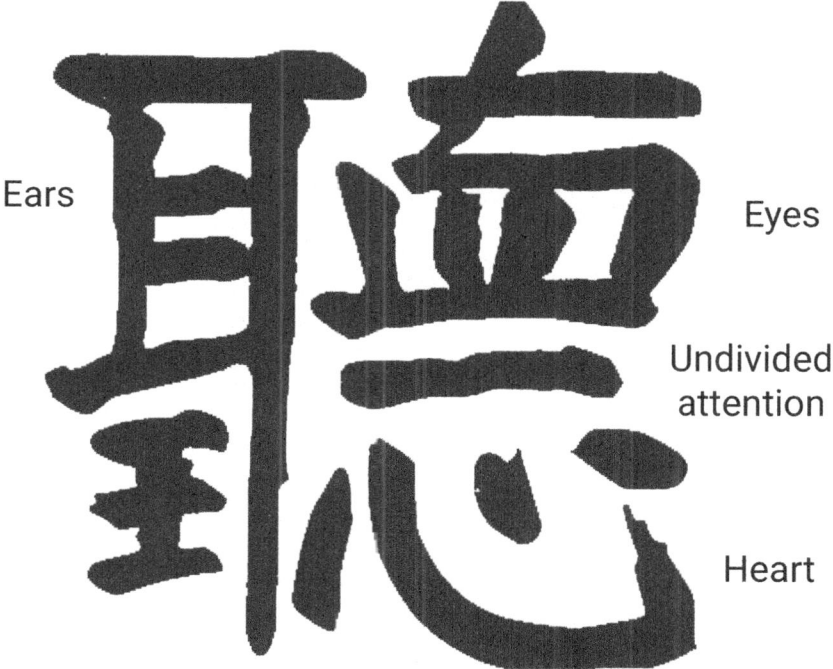

Ears

Eyes

Undivided
attention

Heart

Fig. 1

Made in the USA
Middletown, DE
13 April 2023